DATE DUE

VOICES
above the Crowd

VOICES
above the Crowd

Life-styles of fifteen
outstanding Americans

by Daniel R. Taylor

WORD BOOKS, Publisher

Waco, Texas · London, England

Library of Congress catalog card number: 70–135116
Printed in the United States of America

Grateful acknowledgment is made for the use of the following copyright material:

Bobby Richardson, *The Bobby Richardson Story*. Old Tappan, N. J.: Fleming H. Revell Co., 1965. Used by permission.

J. Edgar Hoover, "Why I Go To Church." Nashville: Tidings Materials for Christian Evangelism. Used by permission.

All Scripture quotations, unless otherwise marked, are from the King James Version of the Bible.

Quotations marked RSV are from the Revised Standard Version of the Bible, copyright 1946 and 1952 by the Division of Christian Education of the National Council of Churches of Christ in the United States.

Quotations marked Phillips are from *The New Testament in Modern English* by J. B. Phillips. New York: The Macmillan Company, © J. B. Phillips, 1958.

The quotation marked Moffatt is from *The Bible, A New Translation* by James Moffatt. New York: Harper and Row, copyright 1954, by James Moffatt.

First Printing—October 1970
Second Printing—January 1971

To Beverly,
who is to me
a sympathetic and devoted
"voice above the crowd"

Contents

Acknowledgments

To Mrs. Virginia Fields, who combines so admirably the secretarial qualities of looking like a girl, acting like a lady, thinking like a man, and working like a dog.

To Miss Eugenia Price, one of those who responded to the questionnaire, for her encouragement and kind words.

To all of the gracious people who took the time and effort to respond to our questionnaire, including Misses Eugenia Price and Helen Steiner Rice, Senators Mark Hatfield and Charles Percy, Messrs. Pat Boone, Edward N. Cole, Conrad N. Hilton, Jerome Hines, J. Edgar Hoover, W. Maxey Jarman, Thomas W. Landry, J. C. Penney, Bobby Richardson, Norman Rockwell, and Charles M. Schulz.

To Mrs. Helen White for the splendid job she has done in typing the manuscript.

Contributors

PAT BOONE — Singer, Actor, Recording Artist, Motion Picture and Television Star, Author

EDWARD N. COLE — President, General Motors Corporation; Mechanical Engineer

MARK O. HATFIELD — U. S. Senator; Governor of Oregon; Educator

CONRAD N. HILTON — Hotel Owner and Executive, Hilton Hotels International

JEROME HINES — Opera Singer, Metropolitan

J. EDGAR HOOVER — Director, Federal Bureau of Investigation

W. MAXEY JARMAN — Business Executive, GENESCO Inc.

THOMAS W. LANDRY — Head Coach, Professional Football, Dallas Cowboys

J. C. PENNEY — Merchant; Founder, J. C. Penney Co., Inc.

CONTRIBUTORS

CHARLES H. PERCY — *U. S. Senator; President, Bell and Howell Co.*

EUGENIA PRICE — *Author, Religious Non-fiction and Fiction*

HELEN STEINER RICE — *Inspirational Poet, Gibson Greeting Cards, Inc.*

BOBBY RICHARDSON — *Athlete; Baseball, New York Yankees*

NORMAN ROCKWELL — *Illustrator, Artist*

CHARLES M. SCHULZ — *Cartoonist, "Peanuts"*

Preface

The society in which we live could be characterized as a materialistic one. We are concerned about our physical selves—that they be trim, fashionably attired, reasonably healthy, well-trained in skill and talent, suitably housed amid pleasing furnishings, comfortably transported, appropriately entertained, pleasantly relaxed, demandingly challenged, provocatively interesting to others, highly ranked in status, fulfilled in expression and succulently fed.

And though it is true that we must have this "bread," still practically all of us, at least in our more reflective moments, are aware that it is also true that "man doth not live by bread alone."

It is in the quest for the challenging exterior that many become aware of the necessity for an adequate interior.

Long ago the prophet Isaiah had reference to this when he said, "Lengthen your ropes and strengthen your stakes." It is the figure of the camper who is putting up his tent. If he lengthens his ropes, he must strengthen his stakes or the wind is apt to play havoc with his tent.

The application is obvious. The challenging times in which we live have caused most of us to lengthen our ropes almost to their capacities. Unless there is a corresponding strengthening of our inward fortifications, the results ultimately will be disastrous.

Of course, we cannot use God to attain our own materialistic goals. But sometimes in the realization of our own inadequacies, we are brought to the place where we cease trying to use God and begin trying to be used of Him. It is then that we begin to find forgiveness, inner strength, satisfaction and purpose through His son, Jesus Christ.

In an endeavor to discover how some outstanding Americans have "strengthened their stakes," a questionnaire was mailed out by the writer. The responses were diverse and interesting. Some made no reply; others in a courteous way said, "Thanks, but no thanks"; others sent copies of addresses, pamphlets, and books; and still others (bless their hearts) completed the questionnaires and returned them.

The process of corresponding with these people was an exciting one. Even more important, it yielded valuable viewpoints about life and ways of facing life successfully.

The questionnaire contained ten questions. The ten parts of this book are based upon the responses to those ten questions. The last quotation of each part will be from the Bible, which we consider to be the ultimate source of correct viewpoints.

These insights are shared with you, the reader, with the prayer that they may help you "strengthen your stakes" as you "lengthen your ropes."

DANIEL R. TAYLOR

I. Priority

"First things first" is a time-worn statement familiar to all of us. But before we write it off because it is trite, let us remember that many of our most common expressions are common and worn *because* they are relevant, because they meet human need.

A few years ago, I was in an Eastern city attending a convention. There I was intrigued by the tiny buses, the "jitneys" that were used to shuttle conventioneers between meeting places.

The "jitneys" were plentiful but they were small. Almost instantly every seat would be filled. When, several times in succession, I had failed to secure a seat and had had to wait for another opportunity to find one, it occurred to me that those small public transporters of people were remarkably like individual lives.

All of us, from the most gifted to the plainest, like the midget buses, are beset by limitation. Each person has limited time, talent, money, and capacity. If we, like the "jitneys," indiscriminately receive what comes on a "first come, first serve" basis, many of life's most significant opportunities and choices will be crowded out by secondary matters.

So, one is reminded that the ancient bit of wisdom, "first things first," is more than a cliché. It is a timely exhortation to you and me to make room on our "jitneys" for primary matters.

But the question arises, what "things" should be first?

This was the thrust of the first item on the questionnaire.

The question was stated as follows:

With the multitude of things claiming one's attention today, how do you determine your priorities in living?

EUGENIA PRICE: *I believe God teaches us right selectivity, but eight years ago, I determined to slow down—to learn to say no, to schedule time enough to be alone with God— to fill up again from fourteen years of keeping a hectic writing and speaking schedule. People* always come before organizational demands to me. If one can learn how to be misunderstood, it is simpler to live sanely, to be rightly selective. Everyone is expendable. I have faced the fact that I am a private person. First priority where my time is concerned is "time alone." I'm no good otherwise. Where people have needs, my first efforts go toward the elderly. They are far more important than we think!

CONRAD N. HILTON:

A fostering of personal relationships, family and friends, associates and neighbors, should receive maximum attention and application in life. Then there are the important priorities stemming from a correct choice of vocation, a life's work in which each large or small addition to one's basic knowledge and understanding is a fulfilling pursuit. Next, a man's valuable leisure time will demand of him the utmost scrutiny. Here, balance and judgment are the keys; adequate relaxation, food for the mind, contemplation and prayer, social concern, games, philosophy and literature, with each experience considered from the perspective of worthiness and growth of the whole person and his role among men.

THOMAS W. LANDRY:

By listing in order of importance the things claiming one's attention. In my life, these priorities are:

1. My faith in Christ
2. My family
3. Dallas Cowboys

MARK O. HATFIELD:

In my view the most important facet of life is the developing of proper relationships with God and with your fellowman. With this in mind my priorities are: (1) developing a proper relationship with the Lord, (2) developing a proper relationship with my family, (3) the maintaining of a proper relationship with my closest associates in the building of Christ's kingdom and

*in my activities in the political
field.*

PAT BOONE: *I am determined that God is to
be first in my life, and I try to
make every decision by asking
what God wants me to do. When
the demands on my time inter-
rupt what I believe God expects,
there must be changes made!*

CHARLES M.
SCHULZ: *I try to choose those things that
are best suited to the whole
family, and least likely to offend.*

JEROME HINES: *By prayer.*

W. MAXEY
JARMAN: *I do not know that there is any
system for determining priorities
in life. It of course becomes a
matter of judgment, and decisions have to be made constantly,
almost subconsciously, as to what
must receive time and attention
and what must be passed up. If
a person is living close to God,
undoubtedly the Holy Spirit will
help him make decisions.*

HELEN STEINER
RICE: *Show me the way,
    not to fortune and fame,
Not how to win laurels*

[21]

> or praise for my name—
> But Show Me The Way
>   to spread "The Great Story"
> That "Thine is The Kingdom
>   and Power and Glory."

NORMAN
ROCKWELL:

My work comes first.

J. C. PENNEY:

I decided that the "one more thing needed" was for me to learn how to give myself over to God's purpose. I became convinced that in order to take my faith seriously, I must find God's will for the use of the talents I possess and experience I have had.[1]

BOBBY
RICHARDSON:

I take my stand on a Bible verse that has strengthened and challenged me because I know to claim it means a completely surrendered life: "I am crucified with Christ; nevertheless I live, yet not I, but Christ liveth in me; and the life which I now live in the flesh I live by the faith of the Son of God, who loved me, and gave himself for me" (Galatians 2:20). I realize simply that it is God who has given me the ability, the opportunity and certainly any supposed earthly glory that might come through playing ball. I enjoy the sport I am in, but only because I feel that this is where God would have me serve Him.[2]

A man's first responsibility before God is to his immediate family.[3]

But seek ye first the kingdom of God, and his right-eousness; and all these things shall be added unto you.

MATTHEW 6:33

II. Discouragement

You may or may not be a fisherman but I strongly suspect that you can identify with Simon Peter when he said, "We have fished all night and caught nothing."

All of us have known the horrible frustration of failure, of disappointment, and of shattered dreams.

Discouragement is forever trying to thrust its downcast head into our lives.

A statement in the Old Testament tells us "David encouraged himself. . . ." Is this not a fascinating statement? We find ourselves wondering how he did it. We need to learn David's secret. We need a plan, a philosophy, a process whereby we can lift our spirits when they seem bent on depression. Is there some means of coping effectively with discouragement?

DISCOURAGEMENT

The second item of the questionnaire was:

One of the common problems in life is discouragement. How do you deal with it?

EUGENIA PRICE:

Common sense. I believe we become discouraged mainly because we are overly tired most of the time. (Answer to that under No. 1.) Time alone. I have tried this for eight years. It works. I am seldom discouraged now, because I am seldom tired. I also take Jesus quite literally: He said we are to take our days and the trouble and bumps of those days one at a time. I try to do this. I also attempt to be realistic about myself and my abilities; that is, I do not expect more from me than I am capable of delivering. When I was a new Christian I was convinced God would not "make it" without exhausting me in the process. This is nonsense. He makes it all right.

CONRAD N. HILTON:

To remain a discouraged person is nothing more than dwelling in a kind of despair, and as such the impulse should be expelled from the mind as soon as it is recognized. Life has its sad moments, its ups and downs, and I think that these more disappointing occasions can be readily combated. First, a clear conscience and a sense of righteousness in all of one's activities precludes any great somberness in life. Secondly, in the most depressing moments, work, prayer and faith, and a regard for our relatively ideal circumstance compared with the less fortunate in the world, should completely rout any dismay or lingering discouragement we might have. We must always be conscious of the fact that pitying ourselves is a great weakness.

THOMAS W. LANDRY:

In order to overcome discouragement, you must have a purpose in life. My purpose is living a life for Christ. In moments of discouragement, turning to prayer and Scripture reading gives great comfort. Besides this, I believe you must set definite goals and keep focusing on them.

MARK O. HATFIELD: "Have no anxiety about anything, but in everything by prayer and supplication with thanksgiving let your requests be made known to God. And the peace of God which passes all understanding, will keep your hearts and your minds in Christ Jesus" (Philippians 4: 6, 7, RSV).

PAT BOONE: I learned long ago that by reading the Bible and praying I could find renewed strength in spite of disappointments and discouragement.

CHARLES M. SCHULZ: Sometimes, I just get discouraged, but I have a feeling that time gradually heals all hurts and wounds.

JEROME HINES: By prayer.

W. MAXEY JARMAN: How can a real Christian permit discouragement, except perhaps as to his own failures in living up to what he should do? And the answer there is to confess your faults to the Lord and let Him give you a clean slate so that you can start over again. We live in an evil world but God's power will overcome.

HELEN STEINER RICE:

Sometimes I grow very discouraged with my own inadequacy and inability to properly handle all the things that go over my desk. But at times like that, I remind myself that I am just a small FOOT SOLDIER in the ARMY OF THE LORD, and He did not ask me to win the BATTLE alone. But I think we all get the idea that we can change the world single-handedly. I have had many frustrations and discouragements along the way, but I know that is the fabric of which life is woven. I accept them all as GIFTS from God . . . not always with grace . . . but I am learning.

NORMAN ROCKWELL:

I get depressed sometimes but I just work out of it by working.

J. C. PENNEY:

. . . May I recommend a prayer . . . It reads: 'I will try this day

to live a simple, sincere, and se-
rene life, repelling promptly every
thought of discontent, anxiety,
discouragement, impurity, self-
seeking, cultivation of cheerful-
ness, magnanimity, charity, and
the love of holy silence; exercising
economy in expenditure, generos-
ity in giving, carefulness in con-
versation, diligence in appointed
service, fidelity to every trust, and
a child-like faith in God." [1]

. . . But David encouraged himself in the Lord his
God.

I Samuel 30:6

III. Avocation

An old miner once explained to a visitor, "I let my mules spend one day a week outside the mines to keep them from going blind."

Life can become very "daily" and routine. Most of us need some sideline or hobby to which we can turn regularly to keep us from "going blind" to the challenges, adventures, and possibilities of our regular vocations.

The third question was:

Do you have a hobby or a sideline to which you turn periodically for a change of pace from your regular routine? Describe. Do you find it helpful? Explain.

EUGENIA PRICE: *I would have to say I do not have. My work is my dear delight. Only* answering my mail seems like "work" to me. But, I do futz around in my yard some, ride a bicycle for exercise (force myself to do this), and, when I am not writing books, I am reading them. My need for a hobby seems almost nil. I have no particular explanation for it, except to say that in the almost twenty years I have been a Christian, I have not been bored. I was always bored before.

CONRAD N. HILTON:

In the realm of leisure time, I find listening to music a most refreshing pastime, I enjoy playing golf, and dancing has provided its light-hearted and very pleasant moments. However, since I am gregarious by nature, I enjoy nothing more than the friendships and visits of my family and acquaintances, with a very special emphasis on my sons and grandchildren. As a result of watching my grandchildren grow up, being around all these young people has kept me young in spirit and given me an insight into their generation. I enjoy challenging their eager and ambitious minds, and they are certainly a group for which I have the greatest hope.

THOMAS W. LANDRY:

My hobby is golf. Other than an extended vacation, golf gives me the most relaxation. Three or four hours out in the fresh air, concentrating on a white ball, seems to relieve you of most of your problems.

MARK O. HATFIELD:

I don't of myself have a special hobby as I find a great deal of interest in every facet of life. When I am not engaged in my work (which I enjoy very much), my family and all the activities that surround our home take first place.
My wife and I have a great deal of interest in the collecting of antiques, in reading, and in gardening.

PAT BOONE:

I enjoy many hobbies, particularly those involving athletics. I try to play basketball during lunch hour every day.

AVOCATION

CHARLES M. SCHULZ:
Golf—Reading—Although, I enjoy my regular routine too much really to need to break it.

JEROME HINES:
Composing.

W. MAXEY JARMAN:
As to changing pace from regular routine, my whole life is so involved in change that I rarely feel the need for any particular change. I do a lot of traveling, I do a lot of reading. I meet with a lot of different kinds of people, and I try to keep an open mind so that I'll get new ideas from every source.

HELEN STEINER RICE:
I just want to say to you that with me this is a vocation, an avocation, and a dedication. And while I work for a commercial company, it is because I must have a channel through which I can reach people. So, I am happy to make PROFITS FOR GIBSON that I may make PROPHETS FOR GOD.

NORMAN ROCKWELL:
I have no hobbies. Just paint every day all year long.

J. C. PENNEY:
I have never had any hobbies, as such; I have diversified interests.

[33]

As an avocation, I have a farm in Dutchess County, New York, where I breed purebred Aberdeen Angus cattle. I have over six hundred head of cattle on my farm. I have always felt that it has been my closeness to nature and my cattle breeding that have accounted so much for my good health.[1]

"Come ye apart and rest a little while."

MARK 6:31

IV. Motivation

What causes two members of the same family to follow diverse courses in life? What causes one brother to be a Jacob and the other an Esau? What causes one person to work with zest and vigor while another on the same job merely "punches the clock"?

What causes one to work harder playing golf than at his vocation and another to work much harder at his vocation than at golf? What causes one person to succeed in a conspicuous manner while another from similar environment fails miserably?

Motivation is a fascinating study, and it was the subject of the fourth question in the questionnaire.

One who has attained a position in life such as yours must have a strong motivation. What do you consider to be the strongest motivating force in your life? Explain.

[35]

EUGENIA PRICE: *To write up to the limits of my ability. This is one of the main reasons I put the lid down on speaking engagements—I was not allowing myself enough time for careful writing. I feel the central emphasis in all of life should be the potential we have of discovering something of what God is really like. Believing in books as I do, I would say my motivating force is to learn to communicate God. You see, knowing Him has made the difference between life and dullness to me. I am affiliated with no special group—Jesus Christ is my polestar. My motivation: discovering more and more of what He is like. I find this central drive increases my enjoyment of everything! Too many of us are* UNAWARE. *He is the source of awareness.*

CONRAD N. HILTON: *The strongest motivation in my life is to do the best I can, and this directly relates to what I believe my God expects of me. Every person is given certain abil-*

ities, and he had better develop himself to the utmost. We can only discover what we are really capable of by work—hard work. I consider this to be life's primary calling: the great responsibility to achieve, to accomplish, and to persist in even greater accomplishment. In this sense, work is prayer, and I must not disappoint the faith which God has placed in me by endowing me with life, a mind and will to do! Such is my motivation; and it also follows that fulfillment through achieving and being of benefit to my fellow human beings cannot help but be of great personal satisfaction.

THOMAS W. LANDRY:

Pride is the strongest motivating force in my business. An athlete who is not proud of his accomplishments, regardless of the odds, will never reach the top. He can come close if God has given him enough natural ability, but pride gets him over the "hump."

MARK O. HATFIELD:

The strongest motivation of my life I believe comes from the realization that I can actually have a personal relationship with God and through His love develop the stronger bonds with my fellow human beings. The motivating force in my life is summed up in Matthew 22:37: "Thou shalt love the Lord thy God with all thy heart, and with all thy soul, and with all thy mind."

PAT BOONE:

The strongest motivating force in my life is determination to use the opportunities which I have to the glory of God.

CHARLES M. SCHULZ:

I try to make my work good in the creative and artistic sense. I am driven by pride along those lines.

JEROME HINES:

Jesus Christ.

W. MAXEY JARMAN:

I doubt if anyone can really explain the motivating forces in his life. I have felt that there have been certain psychological compulsions upon me to use the ability that I have had, to use my

time well, and to fulfill the re-
sponsibilities that have been
placed upon me. But I really
could not analyze very effectively
what have been motivating forces
in my life.

HELEN STEINER
RICE:

I do not think of myself as a success, or as a writer, or as a poet. I
just think of myself as another
worker in GOD'S VINEYARD. The
phenomenal sale of my books and
writings is not due to anything
special about me or my way of
living. It is just because people all
over the world, under God's direction, have seen their own souls
reflected in the words that I have
borrowed from God. When I
read the mail that comes in to my
desk, I can only realize this is a
MODERN MIRACLE.

NORMAN
ROCKWELL:

I do not know what is my "motivating force." I just love to paint.
It is my only form of expression.

J. C. PENNEY:

We have been finding out that by
an immutable law the spirit and
practice of service underlie even

material success. As a seed must be buried in the cold, damp earth before its blossoms can come forth into the sunshine, so every success must be preceded by sacrifice. Self-denial is the basic requirement for accomplishment in any field or endeavor. The law is inescapable. This I know not only in theory but from personal experience. Success comes only to those who will follow the hard road and who are willing to sacrifice everything except honor to achieve their goal.

Success, first of all, is a matter of the spirit. When I see a young man or a young woman identifying himself or herself so closely with his or her work that the closing hour passes unheeded, I recognize the beginning of success. Such young people are doing more than is required of them— that is, more than the employer requires—but not more than their conscience demands.

If it is possible to live the Christian life at any point it should be possible to live it in all relationships of one's life. A man should first ask himself, when he faces a question of business choice, "Is this worthy of my best?" If the answer is "yes," he should go into it, not only retaining his self-respect, but also holding fast to the highest Christian standards.[1]

There is no doubt in my mind that whatever success I have enjoyed is due to the training my parents gave me! Many times when I have been up against it, my father's last words, about me, before his death have come back to me like a clarion call. These words were: "Jim will make it. I like the way he has started out."

When he said those words, it was because he knew that he had given me the most valuable asset any man can have—a high standard of values and a strong religious faith.[2]

BOBBY
RICHARDSON:

I hadn't gone into baseball to try to be rich or famous. I'd become a Christian at fourteen and believed that my life's purpose was

to please God. I had a lot to learn
about the Lord, and still do, but
I'd always felt that my interest in
the sport had been given to me by
God and I was in it to glorify
Him.[3]

Another question sure to be asked
was how my teammates reacted
to my Christian convictions. I
believe my answer is true in baseball or anywhere else in life. Any
man will command respect if he
takes a stand and backs it up with
his life. If the life doesn't reflect
the testimony, however, the result
is contempt.[4]

*Yet, my brothers, I do not consider myself to have
"arrived," spiritually, nor do I consider myself already
perfect. But I keep going on, grasping ever more
firmly that purpose for which Christ grasped me."*

PHILIPPIANS 3:12–13, Phillips

V. God

Do you believe in God? If you and I were to knock on every door in almost any community in America and ask that question, I suspect in virtually every case, we would receive an unequivocal "yes" answer. Indeed, a recent survey revealed that 97 percent of the American population believes in God.

However, the sharply increasing crime rates, indications of rising immorality, a widening "credibility gap" in high places and low, and a failure to identify in any meaningful way with the purposes of God by millions of people would tend to diminish the importance of an affirmative answer to the question.

Perhaps a more appropriate and revealing question would be "What do you believe about God?" Some think of Him as a "doting grandfather" or a ruthless and relentless tyrant, or a celestial scorekeeper, or a divine killjoy, or a remote impersonal influence.

Such small and inaccurate concepts of God are not likely to improve the crime, morality, credibility, or identification of people with the purpose of God in contemporary America.

Fortunately there are many people in our country who know and serve an infinitely bigger, nobler, greater, more loving, merciful, and powerful God than some of their misguided and deluded friends.

The fifth item of the questionnaire asked:

Do you believe in a personal God one can know? If so, how do you feel one can know Him? Can you give something of your own personal experience with God?

EUGENIA PRICE: *Indeed I do. There is only one way to know God and that is through Jesus Christ, His Son. That sounds ultra-orthodox. I insist upon no doctrinal emphasis except this. The day I became a believer, the friend with me almost dared me to speak to Him. I did and He was there. I am convinced that all the barriers are on our side. God has done all that even God can do to knock them* down from His side! Anyone can come to know enough of the intentions of God through a personal encounter with Jesus Christ to live adequately to anything. I did not say to live with a perpetual pious smile on one's face—I said "adequately."

CONRAD N.
HILTON:

As a Christian, I recognize the divinity of Christ, and this loving figure set before us so plainly yet majestically in Scripture is One with whom I can easily identify and communicate. To continually review the life of the Redeemer, to contemplate His words and deeds, is to become familiar with, to love and appreciate His divine person. The benevolent figure of the God-man Christ enables us to understand the Supreme Being within our human capacity to do so. At three particularly crucial points in my career I relied through prayer entirely on God's good graces. I was relatively helpless in these situations, completely at

God's mercy. Without that faith
and without His specific help in
those three instances, I would
not have come through the crises
as I did; I am certain of this—
this I know! It is my own very
personal proof of God's existence.

THOMAS W.
LANDRY:

One can only believe in a personal God that he can focus on.
It is difficult for me to visualize
the God who created this universe; He is bigger than anything
I can imagine. Thank God that
he thought enough of us to send
us Jesus Christ. Jesus gives us a
glimpse of what God is like and
we can focus on God through
Christ.

MARK O.
HATFIELD:

Yes, I do believe that we can
know God. One of the chief
reasons Jesus came, in his own
statement, is "that we might
know the Father who sent him."
In other words, as we get to know
Jesus Christ—who he is, and
what he is like—we thereby know
God in a personal way.

John 14:6–11—this passage

convinces me that Jesus and the Father are one, and that to know Jesus is to know the Father.

PAT BOONE:

I certainly do believe in a personal God, and am convinced that all of life can be shared with Him. This relationship grows out of the revelation of God presented in the Scripture and is in my judgment the point of all of Christianity.

CHARLES M. SCHULZ:

Of course, although I tend to believe it is sacrilegious to say we "know" Him. Especially when we say we know Him better than someone else knows Him. There is a mystery about God which cannot ever be overcome. This is elementary.

JEROME HINES:

You can only know God by accepting Him as He is and not as you want Him to be. He is Creator, Savior and Final Judge, as we can see in the Holy Scriptures. We have to become Sons of God by a decision of will, accepting His sacrifice on the cross

as payment for our sin, and receive His resurrection power
(bodily resurrection) through
the indwelling Holy Spirit. If His
spirit indwells us through our re-
birth, we know him (John 17).

W. MAXEY
JARMAN:

Certainly I believe in a personal
God. I know Him by His revelation to me through His Word, by
prayer, and by the knowledge of
His presence with me at all times.

HELEN STEINER
RICE:

I DO BELIEVE IN PRAYER. I BE-
LIEVE COMPLETELY AND WITHOUT
RESERVATION IN GOD. I BELIEVE
I AM A SHABBY, SMALL, STRUG-
GLING SINNER, but this does not
trouble me too much . . . for I
know that if I ask God to for-
give me, He will . . . and I know
that He died for me, so who am
I to ask Him to explain how His
plan will work. I am very satis-
fied with everything, and I know
that God is the answer to everything. I do not believe anything
ever dies, for in the KINGDOM OF
THE LORD there is nothing lost
forever . . . not a grain of sand,

not a drop of rain, not a crystal of dew. So why would we ever think that God would create man to end in nothingness? I solve my problems one by one, asking nothing of tomorrow . . . only that GOD'S WILL BE DONE.

J. C. PENNEY: The glimmerings of conviction that it was not enough for men to be upright and moral were growing upon me when another fiery ordeal came my way—one that almost broke me physically and mentally. It brought me to a new sense of humility and dependence upon God; and, as happens when man reaches his extremity, and sincerely and earnestly seeks God's aid, it was forthcoming. A light illumined my soul. I cannot otherwise describe it and never could I be the same man again.

I came to see that I must take still another step—that I must give myself over to God's purpose. It is difficult to find words which express what happened. I became convinced that in order to take the practice of Christian principles to its ultimate end, I must find God's will for the use of the talents I possessed and experiences I had had. I awakened to the realization that knowing God's will was not easy, that one must seek it through prayer, and that our prayers are often strained through our own selfish desires and colored by our own wills, so that one must keep returning to the Source of all life in order to be renewed.[1]

BOBBY
RICHARDSON:

Mr. Simpson used the best-known verse in the Bible to make salvation plain—John 3:16: "For God so loved the world, that he gave his only begotten Son, that whosoever believeth in him should not perish, but have everlasting life."

All mankind was sinful and in need of God's mercy and salvation. Did we know—Willie Ann, Inez, and I—that we too were sinful? No one had ever put the question to me directly before, and it caused some self-examination.[2]

. . . Those thoughts flashed through my mind as Pastor Simpson sat in our living room that day and asked us quite simply if we believed that we were sinners in the eyes of God. It was a penetrating question. God's Word said we were. He read Romans 3:23: "For all have sinned, and come short of the glory of God." All. That included me. I didn't feel particularly like classifying myself that way. But the pastor had put the Word of God before me and I could believe it or not. I chose to believe it. "Yes," I said, "I'm a sinner." [3]

. . . Those facts were not new to me. What was new was hearing them from someone who told me face to face that they applied to me! I had believed without difficulty that Jesus had died for the sins of the whole world. But had he died for my sins? It was quite a different question.

Once again my answer came and this time I would spend the rest of my life discovering its importance.

"Yes," I said, "Jesus died for me."

My sisters gave the same answer. The pastor bowed his head and asked God to bless us. Then, after instructing us to read our Bibles regularly and to pray, he left.[4]

There would be a "lull" of several years before I would experience any real spiritual growth. But I know now, looking back, that in the living room of my home that day, in the simple act of believing that Jesus died for me, the power of God's Word began to work. I saw for the first time really, that a live, flesh-and-blood Person had suffered an agonizing death because of love for a boy named Robert Richardson.[5]

That day I accepted Jesus Christ as my personal Saviour, and each succeeding year has shown me how important my decision was. It's a wonderful thing to know your sins are forgiven.[6]

Year after year I've been impressed with the great salvation that became mine at fourteen. And more than this, I've come to see that Jesus is my Lord. I'm His personal property and everything I do is His business.

This, then, was the answer to my question after the '64 Series. This is how all things—home runs and costly errors—"work together for good" in my life. It's because He's in charge. It's because I love Him and want to please Him in every possible way.

And that's why He doesn't need my successes to glorify His name. He can do it, perhaps even better, when I fail.[7]

J. EDGAR HOOVER:

Perhaps first and foremost of my reasons for attending church is a certainty—steadily reinforced by observation and experience—that man is a creature incomplete of himself and whose need of God is overwhelming. If man is other than wholly animal—and I conceive him to be the sole living creature endowed with a spiritual nature—does not the spiritual side of his being require nourishment, discipline, cultivation? What better place is there to receive these necessities than in his church?

Man is not beyond good and evil. "As a man thinketh in his heart, so is he." The pattern of man's thoughts necessarily is influenced by his fundamental beliefs. It has been my observation that those who believe in nothing find life a thankless and unhappy quest; those who have faith, a spiritual pilgrimage. The poet says:

From thee, great God, we spring,
    to thee we tend—
Path, motive, guide, original and
    end.[8]

The continuing flood of immorality and crime accompanies an all too evident substitution of a secular, materialistic philosophy for the historic reliance upon divine guidance which has been a cornerstone of our democracy. Is it coincidence that this criminality and this secularism go hand in hand? I do not think so. I think that the criminal flood is an unescapable result of our earlier failure to teach God convincingly to the youthful unfortunates who are our juvenile delinquents of today and who will be our adult criminals of tomorrow. I think that the one sure way to stem the tide and restore our nation to moral sanity is to bring about a return to religion as our guide for daily living.[9]

Faith in man cannot exist without faith in God. Faith in God takes root and grows strong only when it is expressed in service and good works.[10]

Jesus saith unto him . . . he that hath seen me hath seen the Father.

JOHN 14:9

Jesus saith unto him, I am the way . . . : no man cometh unto the Father, but by me.

JOHN 14:6

[55]

VI. Prayer

"God is dead" is a phrase which has been used by some contemporary theologians. Whatever they mean by the phrase, it is one which has brought varying degrees of resentment, indignation, and outright hostility to the hearts, minds, and lips of many who reverence and love God.

The phrase is equally offensive to me. For not only is He alive but He is the source and sustainer of life.

However, insofar as there exists any vital relationship with God—talking to Him, listening to Him, obeying Him, serving Him—in millions of lives, for all practical purposes, He might as well be dead!

When we pray, is there really someone there who listens and responds? Prayer is the theme for Question 6.

[56]

PRAYER

Do you believe in prayer? Do you believe things are accomplished by prayer which otherwise would not occur? Explain. Give personal experience with prayer, if possible.

EUGENIA PRICE:

Yes, I believe in prayer. More accurately, I believe in praying. I feel too many of us put our faith in prayer, rather than in God. To me, there is a subtle difference. Of course, I do not understand how, but I believe "things are accomplished by prayer which otherwise might not occur." Somehow God needs our cooperation in faith. I doubt that He needs it in the sense we think of need—as, for instance, His inadequacy without us—but when we cooperate with Him, we become involved with Him and this is bound to benefit us! Prayer, to me, is being with God.

CONRAD N. HILTON:

According to the quality of our prayer and the disposition of God are our prayers answered. Totally selfish and acquisitive beseeching prayer is less than perfect prayer.

God answers our genuine prayer in numerous ways, ways undoubtedly in many cases beyond our comprehension. Essentially, if we analyze prayer, it is a regard for, a respect, an acknowledgement of and confrontation with our Creator. It is therefore implicitly an act of faith and belief. If man did not pray at all our world would be an unbelieving, alienated one, and discordance and confusion would reign. Our world is half a believing and half an unbelieving world; thus, there are the occasions of turmoil and those peaceably sublime! Every time I pray and receive that feeling of joy and consolation and hopefulness, my prayer has been answered.

THOMAS W. LANDRY:

Yes, I believe in prayer. Prayer is a two-way street—not only are we talking to God, but God is talking with us. True, He is talking in a way we don't fully understand, but our lives are shaped as a result.

MARK O. HATFIELD: When I committed my life to Christ, it was through prayer in private. This prayer was the fulfillment in my search for God. I have felt since that time that I can converse with God personally. Over the years I have observed many things happening in my personal life and career which have convinced me that God answers prayer.

PAT BOONE: I certainly believe that God answers prayer, and have had many experiences in my own life in which problems were solved or a way was opened through difficulties as a result of prayer.

CHARLES M. SCHULZ: Of course.

W. MAXEY JARMAN: Of course I believe in prayer; and I am sure that God, in a mysterious way, permits his power to be called upon in prayer.

HELEN STEINER RICE: I will say that I have many dark days and many disappointments. But if I wait long enough, I know that "ON THE WINGS OF PRAYER" come great compensations.

[59]

J. C. PENNEY:

The stubborn self-will with its pride and complacency which too often controls us will not be overcome; neither will the serenity which God is capable of giving us be forthcoming, without a more intelligent and persistent effort by each of us to come into, and then to abide in, God's presence. What I am trying to say is: —We must learn to pray.

Gradually I have come to realize that knowing God's will is not easy; that one must seek it in humility through prayer and that our prayers are often strained through our own selfish desires and colored by our own wills, so that one must keep returning to the source of all life in order to be renewed.

In discussing prayer let us not forget the need for our actions to conform to the spirit of our prayers. "To pray on rising and then to behave the rest of the day like a pagan is absurd." None of us want to be guilty of this. To avoid the possibility, we need to pray all through the day. The suggestion of one is, "Very brief thoughts, mental invocations, can hold a man in the presence of God. All conduct is then inspired by prayer." Thus when prayer is so understood it becomes a way of life.

This would not deny the value of a set time for prayer. Some would go so far as to urge the value of a specific place. For some time now I have found the spending of fifteen to thirty minutes of each day just before retiring in reading and prayer to be exceedingly helpful—so much so that I would not let the day go by without this practice. I read from one or more of several books which I have found helpful. In this way my last thoughts before going to sleep are on God, on Christ, on my spiritual needs and those of others.[1]

BOBBY RICHARDSON: By itself, of course, prayer has no value. The example of a Christ-filled life must go along with it.

[61]

Children, simple as they are, understand this.[2]

J. EDGAR HOOVER:

Prayer may bring peace of mind. An affirmation of positive values, it is for many the direct means of tapping infinite resources beyond self and replenishing depleted reservoirs of courage, wisdom, and strength.

To sit in the sight of God, acknowledging Him by one's presence and seeking to understand His decrees, can be a vital experience. It may be a time both of giving and of gaining—of humble supplication and of grateful thanksgiving. It may be a time of simple meditation or of glowing inspiration. It may be a period of sharpened perception in which one receives the clearest intimations of immortality. It may be the interval of an instant, yielding an all-encompassing glimpse of a world in which the Christian ethic truly prevails. It may be the briefest span, yet one in which man gains new standards for himself, reassurance in unity with God and fellowman, and higher levels from which to view his little hour on earth.[3]

CHARLES H. PERCY:

As I think over a lifetime, first with my father and mother, after the breakfast dishes had been taken off, we had brought out our lesson books, we'd got our lessons together, and before we'd be off to work or school, and during as many years as I've been married and raising children, we very seldom have missed the chance after breakfast for ten minutes or so for religious service to see how we could relate religion to that day's activities. I don't think I ever had quite the thrill that I had when I walked into the Wednesday morning prayer breakfast and realized that there is a group of twenty to twenty-five senators that meet every Wednesday morning in the Capitol Building at 8:30 for a one-hour service. Each of us takes a turn in giving a sermon, after which every person in that room (and this is a pretty tight schedule for senators) comments for a minute or two on the service that morning. To think that these men, charged with the great responsibility of finding a way to keep our tremendous heritage of freedom in this country, have the feeling that they must start with the knowledge and recognition that we need a source of strength and inspiration beyond ourselves! I think it is something that initiated me to the Senate in such a way that no one else possibly could have appreciated. Party lines broke down immediately as we bowed our heads, as we do each week, and ask for guidance.[4]

You don't get what you want because you don't ask God for it. And when you do ask He doesn't give it to you, for you ask in quite the wrong spirit—you want only to satisfy your own desires.

JAMES 4:3, Phillips

Whatsoever we ask, we receive of Him, because we keep His commandments and do those things that are pleasing in his sight.

I JOHN 3:22

VII. Bible

The Bible is used for many purposes. It adorns coffee tables and mantle pieces. It lists birth and anniversary dates. It serves as a file for such mementos as locks of hair, pressed roses, memorable letters, and so on. It is used as a stimulus to honesty in the taking of oaths. It makes a sentimental and thoughtful birthday or Christmas gift.

There is probably nothing seriously wrong with using the Bible for any of the above purposes. But most of us know that none of these is the primary purpose of the Bible. What is the Bible? What should be its primary use? The Bible serves as the theme for Question 7.

What is your concept of the Bible? Explain. Do you think it is the Word of God to man? Explain.

Do you believe it can help one in daily living? Explain. Do you rely to any extent upon the Bible for daily living? Explain.

EUGENIA PRICE: Yes, I believe the Bible is the Word of God to man. I doubt that I am what some would call a "literalist," but I do not feel this is essential. Of course, the Bible can help us in daily living. But before even the Bible can help, we need to know the GOD of the Bible, and to read and study it—not expecting or even seeking magic formulas—rather expecting and seeking to know more about the nature of the God we follow. What confuses me is the Old Testament. I simply put it aside if I can't balance it out or verify it with the New Testament concept of God in Jesus Christ. I remain terribly excited about the Scriptures, but I also believe, as Stanley Jones says, that "the Word became flesh, not printer's ink."

CONRAD N. HILTON: The Bible has had the most profound philosophical influence in the history of mankind, and only coincidentally—according to the most objective standards—is it by far the greatest piece of literature ever created. To ignore or minimize the importance of the Bible is to deny history, the heights of human inspiration, and one's own relation to the universe. It is the inconceivable imaginations of any number of philosophically diverse human beings. The thread throughout the Bible is the glory of the Word of God. One's long personal familiarity with the Bible renders its various passages memorable. This recall of the words and images of the sacred book continually enriches and fortifies me.

THOMAS W. LANDRY: The Bible is inspired by God. It is God's message to His people. I learned all I know about Christ and his teaching through Bible study. It is responsible for my faith and is a constant source of inspiration.

MARK O. HATFIELD: The Bible is no ordinary book, and it was not given to us to be a storehouse of knowledge. My view of the Bible is that it is the Word of God to man and is to be followed in daily practice and that its precepts are to be obeyed. To paraphrase John 14:21, the man that knows what Jesus wants him to do and does it is the man that loves Him. The greatest significance of the Word of God to me is to meditate on it and apply the truth that I find in it.

PAT BOONE:

I believe that the Bible is the divine Word of God, that it was inspired by Him as the guide for our lives. It is my conviction that our problems grow out of an unwillingness to accept God's Word at face value and a refusal to live by it.

CHARLES M. SCHULZ:

I believe that it is man's concept of the Word of God to man. It is not a book of magic.

JEROME HINES:

The Bible is the Word of God. Guidance that conflicts with Scripture must be rejected. The Bible must be read consistently.

BOBBY RICHARDSON:	*I began using the time on the long road trips for serious Bible study. The more earnestly I pursued it, the more satisfaction and peace resulted.*[1]
CHARLES H. PERCY:	*. . . I know when I had our little prayer at breakfast that morning after the defeat, and we said as we have for so many mornings this wonderful verse from Proverbs, "Trust in the Lord with all thine heart and lean not unto thine own understanding. In all thy ways acknowledge Him, and He shall direct Thy path," the thought came so clearly. Out of defeat maybe we can learn far more than we ever would in victory. Looking back, I was never so grateful for a defeat because we did learn far more.*[2]

All scripture is inspired by God and is useful for teaching the faith and correcting error, for resetting the direction of a man's life and training him in good living.

II TIMOTHY 3:16, Phillips

VOICES ABOVE THE CROWD

As newborn babes, desire the sincere milk of the word [the Bible], *that ye may grow thereby.*

I Peter 2:2

So then faith cometh by hearing, and hearing by the word of God [the Bible].

Romans 10:17

VIII. Church

Varying evaluations always have been placed upon the church by different groups and individuals.

Since its establishment, there always have been those who loved the church, who received conscious blessing, enrichment, and power from being active in its mission. There always have been those dedicated and faithful to the church who have given even sacrificially in prayer, money, time, talent, compassion, and energy to help accomplish its goals and purposes. There always have been those who have sung its praises.

On the other hand, the church has never been without its critics and skeptics. Even the pioneers of the church, those who walked with the Lord Himself, were maligned and condemned as was He.

Every generation of church members since that

time has endured its share of criticism. Some of it doubtless has been justified; some of it has been unfair.

Probably no generation of churchmen has been more the object of analysis, examination, skepticism, and ridicule than the contemporary one. And alas, surprising as it may seem, much of the criticism comes from within the institutional church.

Are the problems to be found in the church, in the minds and hearts of the critics, or perhaps partially in both? In not a few cases, churchmen have become introspective and have begun asking some of the questions which form Item 8 in the questionnaire.

Do you believe the contemporary church is effective? Explain. Do you believe it is relevant? Explain. What about the contemporary church could you commend? What improvements would you like to see made in it? Is the church important in your life? Explain.

EUGENIA PRICE: *I assume you are asking about the organized church—not the Body of Christ. It would be ideal if those two were synonymous. At this point on my journey, I do not believe they are necessarily. The Body of Christ is impregnable. The physical, man-organized* church is not. I cannot comment on IT as one entity. For almost fourteen years I had the rare experience of speaking in ALL KINDS of churches. Some would not have wanted me had they known where I had just spoken! Therefore, churches vary too much, in my opinion, for a blanket indictment or commendation. I am not church-oriented. My work has prevented it up to now. I have settled in the South where there is no integration in churches. And so I am waiting and observing. I commend ALL that is of love in our churches. Improvements? More love, less organization.

CONRAD N. HILTON: Through history the church has had a sustaining and uplifting effect on the actions of men. The church has helped crystalize and channel our expressions of faith and worship. It represents the oneness and unity of human devotion to which the heart of man is so greatly inclined. The church

[73]

speaks, guides, and authoritatively refines the conscience. Western civilization would not have progressed as it has without the influence of organized religion. The church is relevant today because of the timelessness of the codes and commandments which it promulgates. With some evidence of moral decline and human havoc in this modern age, it is not the church which has failed as some have claimed! Rather it is the individual who has failed to even recognize, much less adhere to, the beautiful, reasoned, and unchanging precepts of the moral order so earnestly conveyed again and again from tens of thousands of pulpits. The church can strengthen freewill; it cannot become the will of men!

THOMAS W. LANDRY:

Yes and no. The church is effective in serving the needs of our older people. It is ineffective in reaching our young people. The church is relevant to social concern, not in spreading the Good News of Jesus Christ. More emphasis should be placed on the teaching of Jesus Christ in Today's English Version to our young people.

MARK O. HATFIELD: Every comment about the church has to draw the distinction between the visible and invisible church. I am impressed by the fact that the church of Christ is one body and that its unseen and unheralded work is going forward throughout the world. My family and I attend regular worship and are participants in our local church. The activities of the church have great significance to us. The work of the church as a fellowship of believers is more relevant today than ever. It holds forth the hope of reconciliation between God and man—and between man and man—that is vital to the continuance of our way of life as we know it.

PAT BOONE: I believe that the Bible presents a picture of the church as God intended it to be, and that it is our continuing responsibility to strive both in doctrine and in personal life in service and in devotion to make the church today what the New Testament church was.

JEROME HINES:

The contemporary, organized church is a disaster. Christ's church—those united in Christ through the Holy Spirit—the true church—are still carrying on His work effectively although they constitute, truly, a remnant.

W. MAXEY JARMAN:

I think the contemporary church is becoming less and less effective, because it is trying to move into social work, reform, and improving the lot of mankind, rather than putting its major emphasis on bringing people to Christ. Of course it's relevant, because human nature is just the same as it was two thousand years ago and the only way in which human nature can be changed from evil to better is by the spiritual power of Christ creating a new person within the individual.

If churches would concentrate on this, I'm sure they would be more effective.

J. C. PENNEY:

Rich is our spiritual heritage and we all owe more than we can ever repay to the church for preserving Christ's teachings, holding together the body of believers, providing a place for religious instruction for ourselves and our children, and giving spiritual leadership in our home communities, in our nation, and to some extent to the whole world.

The layman should give himself, his talents, experience, and support to the church. The church in turn should offer an even greater opportunity for spiritual growth to the layman. Help him see the necessity of bridging the gap between the practical and the spiritual and then counsel him as he proceeds to take the steps day by day which will result in spiritualizing all of his daily contacts.[1]

J. EDGAR HOOVER:

Surely, if one has faith in God, attendance at His church is both a visible affirmation of that faith and an acknowledgment of man's indebtedness to Him. Through his presence, whether it be in the humblest chapel or the loftiest cathedral, man registers his acceptance of the duties and obligations which Christianity imposes and expresses his appreciation for the human dignity which it imparts.[2]

CHARLES H. PERCY:

I found that one of the really most encouraging aspects of American life in the '60s has been the emergence of the church as a dynamic social force. I think churchmen have come a long way in a short time, but I would have to say we've only touched the surface; there is so much more that lay people and clergymen can do, so many other ways in which they can lead. I am therefore not here to eulogize what we have done but to encourage all of us to seek new ways in which we can take religion into American life.

For a long time, I think many

CHURCH

Americans viewed organized religion as not only holy, but holier–than–thou, and that's what young people are saying today. The churches seemed more interested in preaching than practicing—that is what young people tell me on campuses today—more concerned with praying than participating. Ritual obscured reality. A church was successful if its pews and collection plates were full, in the eyes of many. Too often, the people were meant to look up to the church—the church was not meant to come down to the people. The church seemed uninvolved, and as a result, many people could not see their way to becoming involved with the church.[3]

. . . *Upon this rock I will build my church; and the gates of hell shall not prevail against it.*

MATTHEW 16:18

IX. Hope

There is a favorite painting by Watts entitled *Hope*. It is the picture of a woman sitting on the world, a world from which she has suffered much adversity. Her eyes are bandaged, indicating that she cannot see her way. In her hands is a harp, and all of the strings but one are broken. Those broken strings represent her shattered dreams. But the one string left is the string of hope.

Is there any valid hope for a despairing world which has tried so many "strings" and seen them snap? Question 9 asked:

What do you believe is the hope of the world? Explain.

EUGENIA PRICE: *Ultimately—Christ. For today? No pat answer, certainly! This* in no way means that Christ is not hard at work (and success-fully) in His world. I do believe, of course, that it is ALL HIS. We are all in His hands. But some-how Creation is continuing and the direction it can go will be our choice: toward love, brother-hood, trust, or further divisive-ness. I am one of those who in her heart is a pacifist, but who would probably kill to save her-self or a loved one! But I DO NOT SEE THAT WAR ACCOMPLISHES ANYTHING GOOD OR CONSTRUC-TIVE. And I can't help feeling that if we could have more inter-personal relationships with our so-called "enemies," things could change for the better. In a blan-ket statement—love, and love alone, is the only hope.

CONRAD N. HILTON:

One can recognize Christ's re-deeming influence upon the world in the hearts and acts of the true Christian. The world desperately requires a return to moral equilibrium. The Greek philosopher Heraclitus expressed the idea of an ultimate hope or demise of the individual and society with this phrase: "Character is fate." Our circumstance, we ourselves, our world become what we have fashioned from the hours and days of our existence; it can be no other way. The example of Christ and the teachings of the church which can lead each individual to a personal integrity and high-mindedness would seem to be the only meaningful hope for a world such as ours.

THOMAS W. LANDRY:

The only hope of the world is in Jesus Christ. To the Christian, winning the world to Christ is our main purpose.

MARK O. HATFIELD:

Rather than saying, "What is the hope of the world?" I would restate the question, "Who is the hope of the world?" The answer is Jesus Christ. Through Christ we are reconciled to God and to man. Perhaps the greatest privilege in this life is to be a reconciling force through the power of

God. *It is men thus related who can present the hope of the world.*

PAT BOONE: *I believe that the hope of the world is the Lord Jesus Christ.*

CHARLES M. SCHULZ: *God said that He desired mercy and not sacrifice. Man's hope always lies in individual maturity and then in corporate maturity.*

JEROME HINES: *Read Revelation—there is no hope for the world except in Christ's second coming. Our present hope is a salvage operation for individual souls to be snatched from a world in a desperate situation.*

J. C. PENNEY: *I believe in a practical application of the Golden Rule as taught by the Master nearly two thousand years ago. "Therefore all things whatsoever ye would that men should do to you, do ye even so to them: for this is the law and the prophets" (Matthew 7: 12).*

The Golden Rule is one of the most fundamental laws that can be expressed in words. We find it specifically stated in the literature of eleven known religions. Of its origin but little is known, for Christ was not the first to give it expression, though His was the perfect pronouncement.

The Golden Rule is a law of love. It underlies all true religion. Observance of the Golden Rule ensures observance of civil law and carries us past the letter of the law to the spirit which "giveth life." It makes us willing to sacrifice what is commonly called "personal liberty" for the welfare of others and willing to forego indulgences which, however harmless they may seem in our own lives, work ruin in the lives of others.[1]

J. EDGAR HOOVER:

Faith dominated the atmosphere at Independence Hall in Philadelphia where the Declaration of Independence and the Constitution were framed.

Faith is our mainstay in the ideological struggle now raging between the camps of godless communism and human freedom.

And faith remains our strongest bulwark against the criminal and subversive enemies who would destroy our priceless heritage of liberty and justice for all. But faith without work will be of no avail—there must be unity of purpose.

America will continue to progress in dignity and freedom so long as our people cherish liberty and justice and truth and honor God.

Faith in God—that is the fortress of free men.[2]

Law and order are the foundations upon which successful government must stand. Without law and order, society will destroy itself. We must never forget that government cannot favor one group or one special interest over its duty to protect the rights of all citizens. We must constantly guard government against the pressure groups which would crush the rights of others under heel in order to achieve their own ends.[3]

It seems we are never converted en masse to any genuine reform in society, science, religion, morals, or government. There must be a beginning and the time is now. America stands at the crossroads of destiny. It is a common destiny in which we shall all finally stand or fall together. Though we contest with utter vigor for the prevalence of whatever attitudes and policies may possess our souls, may we ever remember that we finally must be all for one and one for all against the vicissitudes of fortune —and perhaps against the world. We are still capable of producing leaders who have the power to move, quicken, and transform their environment, and to awaken an answering thrill of appreciation and support in us who read or hear of their struggles and achievements.[4]

EDWARD N. COLE:

In America, we have developed a system which has elevated the individual from the position of serfdom to that of man in the image of God. No other society has ever placed so much respect, dignity, and dependence on the ideas and energies of the individual. Thus, the individual has the opportunity to earn for himself the rewards of hard work and success. But in so doing, he also contributes to the improvement of our entire population—not just the wealthy and talented ones—but all within our society.[5]

Today, as in the days of Christ, there is a great need for proper Christian conduct and ethics in our business as well as our private lives. Business and industrial concerns, as important influences in our lives and the society in which we live and work, have significant obligations to the ideas of Christian living.

Although I sincerely believe that our businesses, by and large, are fulfilling these obligations, there is always room for improvement. It is the responsibility of all of us—working as individuals and as groups—to seek this improvement. Our lives, our businesses, and the world in which we live will be much the better for it.[6]

For Abraham, when hope was gone, hoped on in faith.

ROMANS 4:18, Moffatt

For thou art my hope, O Lord . . .

PSALM 71:5

X. Retrospect

One of my first speaking engagements as a young minister was at a little frame church in East Texas.

My most vivid memory of that occasion apart from my apprehension at speaking publicly is of a kindly old retired minister with the hoary head of wisdom who was present.

During the Sunday school hour which preceded my speaking, the old gentleman taught the lesson. One of the things I remember among his comments was his statement, "If I had my life to live over, I would be a far greater preacher than I have been."

I know sometimes such statements are empty, meaningless rationalizations, but the fine old man spoke with such fervor and earnestness that I believed him. I did not ask him at the time but I have wondered since just what changes he would have made if he had his life to live over.

This question which I did not ask the elderly minister was submitted in the questionnaire as Item 10.

If you had your life to live over, what changes would you make?

EUGENIA PRICE: *First of all, I would try to learn the necessity for maturity much, much sooner! I am what one would call a "retarded adult." I don't think I even considered growing up until I met Christ at age 33! I would also have read much, much more during the years in which I played too much. I do not feel the years without Christ have been wasted but this is no thanks to me. Only to Him. HE IS TOTALLY A REDEEMER, AND SO HAS MADE REDEMPTIVE USE OF ALL MY GODLESS, HEADSTRONG YEARS. Otherwise, they would have been mostly waste. I should also have paid more attention in history classes. A man or a woman in today's world without a strong sense of history is lost!*

I also wish I had stopped taking myself so seriously long before I did. I wish I had learned that real love is NOT *how the loved one makes me feel, but how I am making the loved one feel. This I could have learned, had I known Christ earlier. There is no other way to learn it that I know about.*

CONRAD N. HILTON:

In terms of the choice of career, I believe I did make the correct decision, and this is so very fundamental to one's contentment and fulfillment in life. I do feel that, given the opportunity, I would seek more education and at an earlier age. I think I would travel more as a young man than I actually did. Travel is a very broadening experience for the young person. I could say that I would have chosen a different age entirely in which to be born; one without depressions and wars and the inconveniences with which we grew up. But this would not be an accurate sentiment. Having come through the many trials and tribulations of the times, I believe I am a better person for having done so.

THOMAS W. LANDRY:

I would hope that I would be able to discover Christ at an earlier age. I was over thirty before I really discovered Him.

MARK O. HATFIELD:

My first impression in answer to this question is that I am so tremendously grateful for what God has done in my life that I cannot imagine it changed, because even through disappointments in my life, it has drawn me closer to my goal in life and that is to know Him better. Perhaps, though, if I were pressed to answer this question, I would say the only thing that I would change is that I would trust God more.

PAT BOONE:

I would try to serve God more fully than in the past.

CHARLES M. SCHULZ:

I'd try to become more involved in things at an earlier age. Shyness and stupidity were my handicaps.

RETROSPECT

JEROME HINES: *The only changes would be in myself. Christ gave me a new nature at the age of 32—I wish it could have been sooner.*

J. C. PENNEY: *I am very often asked that question. I wouldn't want to live my life over again. My life has been full of mistakes. Because of this, it is thought I would profit by my mistakes if I could relive my life. As a matter of fact, if I didn't make these same mistakes I would make others. Any man who has accomplished anything in life has made some mistakes.*

I have fought a good fight, I have finished my course, I have kept the faith.

II TIMOTHY 4:7

Notes

I.

1. J. C. Penney, "The Value of Prayer," p. 2.
2. Bobby Richardson, *The Bobby Richardson Story* (Old Tappan, N. J.: Fleming H. Revell Co., 1965), p. 128. Used by permission.
3. Ibid., p. 102.

II.

1. J. C. Penney, "The Value of Prayer," p. 9.

IV.

1. J. C. Penney, "Christian Principles in Business," p. 3.
2. Ibid., p. 9.
3. Bobby Richardson, *The Bobby Richardson Story*, p. 14.
4. Ibid., pp. 101–2.

V.

1. J. C. Penney, "Christian Principles in Business," pp. 12–13.

NOTES

2. Bobby Richardson, *The Bobby Richardson Story*, p. 38.
3. Ibid., p. 41.
4. Ibid., p. 42.
5. Ibid., p. 43.
6. Ibid., p. 152.
7. Ibid., p. 153.
8. J. Edgar Hoover, "Why I Go To Church" (Nashville: Tidings Materials for Christian Evangelism). Used by permission.
9. J. Edgar Hoover, "The Sunday School—Key to Tomorrow," p. 1.
10. J. Edgar Hoover, Remarks . . . "Sword of Loyola" Award Dinner, p. 5.

VI.

1. J. C. Penney, "The Value of Prayer," pp. 3, 2, 6.
2. Bobby Richardson, *The Bobby Richardson Story*, p. 137.
3. J. Edgar Hoover, "Why I Go To Church."
4. Charles Percy, Address to 18th Anniversary Dinner of Religion in American Life, p. 3.

VII.

1. Bobby Richardson, *The Bobby Richardson Story*, p. 114.
2. Charles Percy, Address to 18th Anniversary Dinner of Religion in American Life, pp. 11–12.

VIII.

1. J. C. Penney, "The Value of Prayer," pp. 7–8.
2. J. Edgar Hoover, "Why I Go To Church."

3. Charles Percy, Address to 18th Anniversary Dinner of Religion in American Life, p. 5.

IX.

1. J. C. Penney, "Christian Principles in Business," pp. 6–7.
2. J. Edgar Hoover, Remarks before The Supreme Council, Thirty-third Degree of The Ancient and Accepted Scottish Rite of Freemasonry, Southern Jurisdiction, U. S. A., in Washington, D. C., October 19, 1965.
3. J. Edgar Hoover, Remarks . . . "Sword of Loyola" Award Dinner, p. 2.
4. Ibid., p. 4.
5. Edward N. Cole, "Christianity in Business," p. 1.
6. Ibid., p. 3.